The Quest

Essential Literary Themes

by Susan E. Hamen

Essential Library

An Imprint of Abdo Publishing | abdopublishing.com

abdopublishing.com

Published by Abdo Publishing, a division of ABDO, PO Box 398166, Minneapolis, Minnesota 55439. Copyright © 2016 by Abdo Consulting Group, Inc. International copyrights reserved in all countries. No part of this book may be reproduced in any form without written permission from the publisher. Essential Library™ is a trademark and logo of Abdo Publishing.

Printed in the United States of America, North Mankato, Minnesota
042015
092015

Cover Photo: Shutterstock Images
Interior Photos: Shutterstock Images, 1, 83; Everett Collection, 13, 15, 17, 21, 23, 75; MGM/Photofest, 18, 86, 88, 94; Everett Historical/Shutterstock, 26, 28; Moviestore/Rex Features/AP Images, 35; Murray Close/Lionsgate/Photofest, 37; Murray Close/Lionsgate/Everett Collection, 39, 40, 43, 45, 51; Lionsgate/Photofest, 48; New Line Cinema/Everett Collection, 57, 63, 67; Warner Brothers/Photofest, 61; New Line Cinema/Photofest, 65; Bakhur Nick/Shutterstock Images, 70; Photofest, 72; Andy D./iStockphoto, 81; Gerry Embleton/North Wind Picture Archives, 91

Editor: Melissa York
Series Designer: Maggie Villaume

Library of Congress Control Number: 2015931190
Cataloging-in-Publication Data

Hamen, Susan E.
The quest / Susan E. Hamen.
    p. cm. -- (Essential literary themes)
Includes bibliographical references and index.
ISBN 978-1-62403-807-5
1. American literature--Themes, motives--Juvenile literature. 2. American literature--History and criticism--Juvenile literature.   I. Title.
810--dc23

2015931190

Contents

1

INTRODUCTION TO
Themes in Literature

*D*o you find yourself drawn to the same types of stories? Are your favorite characters on a quest? Are they seeking revenge? Or are your favorite stories about love? Love, revenge, a quest—these are all examples of themes. Although each story is different, many stories focus on similar themes. You can expand your understanding of the books you read by recognizing the common themes within them.

What Is a Theme?

A theme is a concept or idea that shows up again and again in various works of art, literature, music, theater, film, and other endeavors throughout history. Some themes revolve around a story's plot. For example, a play about a young girl moving away from home and learning the ways of the world would be considered a coming of age story. But themes are not always so easily noticed. For example, a work might have allusions. Allusions are references, sometimes indirect, to other works or historical events. Themes might also relate to specific characters or subjects of a work. For example, many stories present heroes or villains. These common character types are often called archetypes.

How Do You Uncover a Theme?

Themes are presented in different ways in different works, so you may not always be aware of them. Many works have multiple themes. Uncover themes by asking yourself questions about the work. What is the main point or lesson of the story? What is the main conflict? What do the characters want? Where does the story take place? In many cases, themes may not be apparent until after a close study, or analysis, of the text.

What Is an Analysis?

Writing an analysis allows you to explore the themes in a work. In an analysis, you can consider themes in multiple ways. You can describe what themes are present in a work. You can compare one work to another to see how the presentation of a theme differs between the two forms. You can see how the use of a particular theme either supports or rejects society's norms. Rather than attempt to discover the author's purpose in creating a work, an analysis reveals what *you* see in the work.

Raising your awareness of themes through analysis allows you to dive deeper into the work itself. You may begin to see similarities between all creative works that you encounter. You may also improve your own writing by expanding your understanding of how stories use themes to engage readers.

Forming a Thesis

Form your questions about how a theme is presented in a work or multiple works and find answers within the work itself. Then you can create a thesis. The thesis is the key point in your analysis. It is your argument about the work. For example, if you want to argue that the theme of a book is love, your thesis could be worded as follows: Allison Becket's novel *On the Heartless Road* asserts that receiving love is critical to the human experience.

How to Make a Thesis Statement

In an analysis, a thesis statement typically appears at the end of the introductory paragraph. It is usually only one sentence long and states the author's main idea.

Providing Evidence

Once you have formed a thesis, you must provide evidence to support it. Evidence will usually take the form of examples and quotations from the work itself, often including dialogue from a character. You may wish to address what others have written about the work. Quotes from these individuals may help support your claim. If you find any quotes or examples that contradict your thesis, you will need to create an argument against them. For instance: Many critics claim the theme of love is secondary to that of revenge, as the main character, Carly, sabotages the lives of her loved ones throughout the novel. However, the novel's resolution proves that Carly's experience with love is the key to her humanity.

Concluding the Essay

After you have written several arguments and included evidence to support them, finish the essay with

How to Support a Thesis Statement

An analysis should include several arguments that support the thesis's claim. An argument is one or two sentences long and is supported by evidence from the work being discussed. Organize the arguments into paragraphs. These paragraphs make up the body of the analysis.

a conclusion. The conclusion restates the ideas from the thesis and summarizes some of the main points from the essay. The conclusion's final thought often considers additional implications for the essay or gives the reader something to ponder further.

In This Book

In this book, you will read summaries of works, each followed by an analysis. Critical thinking sections will give you a chance to consider other theses and questions about the work. Did you agree with the author's analysis? What other questions are raised by the thesis and its arguments? You can also see other directions the author could have pursued to analyze the work. Then, in the Analyze It section in the final pages of this book, you will have an opportunity to create your own analysis paper.

The Quest

The book you are reading focuses on the theme of the quest, which is also referred to as the journey. The quest is a very popular theme throughout literature, dating back thousands of years. Quest literature includes a hero—willing or unwilling—who is typically called upon to journey to retrieve something or someone and return home. This journey requires great exertion and places trials and obstacles in the path of the hero. Often, he or she is required to travel great distances and is sometimes accompanied by a sidekick or group of companions. Quest literature usually also includes archetypal characters such as wizards, wise men, tricksters, mentors, companions, star-crossed lovers, and devil figures who help or hinder the hero's quest.

Look for the Guides

Throughout the chapters that analyze the works, thesis statements have been highlighted. The box next to the thesis helps explain what questions are being raised about the work. Supporting arguments have also been highlighted. The boxes next to the arguments help explain how these points support the thesis. The conclusions are also accompanied by explanatory boxes. Look for these guides throughout each analysis.

2

AN OVERVIEW OF

The Wonderful Wizard of Oz

L. Frank Baum's *The Wonderful Wizard of Oz,* which was first published in 1900, follows the story of a young girl who is whisked away by a cyclone from her dreary gray existence on the Kansas prairie to the magical and colorful land of Oz. The plot differs in some ways from the familiar 1939 film starring Judy Garland.

Baum's story opens by introducing Dorothy, an orphaned girl who lives with her Aunt Em and Uncle Henry in a sparsely furnished farmhouse in Kansas. As the young girl looks around her, all she sees is gray. Dorothy's small dog, Toto, is the only happiness in her bleak world, and he "saved her from growing as gray as her other surroundings."[1]

The Wonderful Wizard of Oz is the story of Dorothy's quest to the Emerald City and beyond.

Whisked Off to Oz

When Dorothy fails to make it to the storm cellar when a cyclone descends on the family farm, she and Toto are trapped in the house. The cyclone lifts the house and carries it for hours before setting it down in a strange land. Dorothy soon learns her house landed on and killed the wicked Witch of the East. The good Witch of the North comes to help with the fallen house. She believes Dorothy must be a noble sorceress. She welcomes Dorothy to the land of Oz.

Dorothy insists she has no magical powers and asks for assistance in returning to Kansas. The Witch of the North advises Dorothy to travel to the Emerald City, where the Great Wizard of Oz might be able to help her. The good witch instructs Dorothy to follow a road paved with yellow bricks, which will lead her to the city. Dorothy puts on the silver shoes the deceased Witch of the East was wearing and packs a basket with some bread from a cupboard in her house. Then she and Toto start off on their quest for the Emerald City.

The Scarecrow and Tin Woodman

Dorothy soon discovers a scarecrow in a cornfield. She is surprised to hear him speak. Dorothy explains her

Dorothy's first two traveling partners are the Tin Woodman and the Scarecrow.

quest, and the Scarecrow asks if he might join her, explaining that the farmer who made him failed to give him any brains. Dorothy welcomes him to join her, and they set off together.

The next day, the two find a tin woodman in the woods who is rusted firmly in place. Dorothy oils his joints with his oilcan so he can move again. The Tin Woodman asks whether the Wizard of Oz might be able to give him a heart. Dorothy supposes it's a possibility and so gains another traveling companion on her quest.

The Cowardly Lion

The small group travels through a thick forest and comes upon the Cowardly Lion, who tries to scare them but fails. Ashamed, he explains to the group that he has no courage, which makes his life very unhappy. After hearing the purpose of the others' quest, he decides to join them and ask Oz for courage.

As the group travels on, it becomes apparent the Scarecrow, Tin Woodman, and Cowardly Lion truly do possess the virtues they seek, although they don't realize it. The Scarecrow devises plans to overcome obstacles, the Tim Woodman can't bear to hurt animals, and the Cowardly Lion bravely stands up to other beasts to protect his companions.

On their quest, they meet residents of the land of Oz who assure them the Wizard is quite powerful. One man warns Dorothy the Wizard does not permit anyone to see him. "We must try," says Dorothy, "or we shall have made our journey for nothing."[2]

The Emerald City

The group strays off the path and into a field of poppies. The scent of the poppies lulls Dorothy, the Cowardly Lion, and Toto into a deep sleep. With the help of some talking field mice, the companions all escape the field and eventually arrive at the front gate of the Emerald City. The gatekeepers let them in, but the group is

Dorothy needs her friends' help when she falls asleep in the field of poppies.

required to wear spectacles to protect their eyes from the bright glory of the city. Everything in the city, from the water to people's skin, is green.

One by one, the travelers see the Wizard of Oz, who appears to each of them in a different form. He tells them he will help them only if they kill the wicked Witch of the West. Disheartened, the foursome sets out to try to vanquish the wicked witch.

Pursuing the Wicked Witch

The Witch of the West sees the group coming and sends wolves to destroy them. However, the Tin Woodman wields his ax and kills them. The witch then sends a

Dorothy defeats the Witch of the West by melting her with water.

flock of wild crows and a swarm of black bees. The Scarecrow and Tin Woodman defeat them because the crows' beaks and bees' stingers do not harm them.

Enraged, the witch summons the Winged Monkeys using her enchanted Golden Cap. The monkeys drop the Tin Woodman over sharp rocks and pull the straw from the Scarecrow. They then capture the others. They fly the Lion, Dorothy, and Toto to the witch's castle. The witch locks up the Lion and starves him. She notices

Dorothy wears the enchanted Silver Shoes and forces her to clean the castle as she contemplates how to get the shoes from the girl. Dorothy sneaks food to the Cowardly Lion at night as several days pass.

When the witch trips Dorothy and steals one shoe, Dorothy becomes mad and throws mop water on her. The witch quickly begins melting. With the witch dead, the Winkies, a race of Oz-landers the witch had enslaved, are now free. Reunited, the group summons the Winged Monkeys using the Golden Cap, and the monkeys fly them to the Emerald City.

Oz the Great Humbug

The friends are disappointed when the Wizard of Oz makes them wait day after day to see him. When Oz finally agrees to see them, they discover he is not a powerful wizard but rather an old man hiding behind a screen. He confesses he's simply using trickery to make people believe he has powers.

The Wizard explains he was once part of a circus in Omaha, Nebraska. He was blown to the Land of Oz in his hot air balloon years before. Since he came from the sky, the people of Oz thought he must be a great wizard. He then built the Emerald City and ruled over it. The city is not really green, but because everyone wears green spectacles, it looks green.

Up, Up, and Away

Oz decides the only way to grant Dorothy's wish is to sew a new hot air balloon and attempt to fly her back to Kansas himself. On the day of the launch, Dorothy misses the balloon when Toto runs after a kitten. Unable to stop the balloon's ascent, she watches as the Wizard of Oz flies off, along with her chance of returning to Kansas.

The Scarecrow suggests summoning the Winged Monkeys to fly her over the desert that borders Oz. However, the monkeys explain they cannot leave the country. A soldier suggests that Glinda, the Witch of the South, might be able to help Dorothy. The Scarecrow, Lion, and Woodman all come with Dorothy.

Glinda the Good Witch

The group meets the beautiful Glinda. Glinda informs Dorothy she always had the power to go home with the enchanted Silver Shoes. "If you had known their power you could have gone back to your Aunt Em the very first day you came to this country."[3] However, Dorothy's new

Glinda helps Dorothy see she's had the power she needs the whole time.

friends point out that if Dorothy had not come along, they would still be stuck in their own woeful situations.

Glinda teaches Dorothy how to use the shoes. The girl hugs and kisses her travel partners and tearfully says her good-byes. She then clicks her heels three times and declares, "Take me home to Aunt Em!"[4]

Instantly Dorothy is whirled through the air and deposited on the broad Kansas prairie. She sees a newly built farmhouse and notices she has lost her Silver Shoes. She runs toward Aunt Em, who cries, "My darling child! Where in the world did you come from?"[5]

"From the Land of Oz," Dorothy explains. "And oh, Aunt Em! I'm so glad to be at home again!"[6]

3

Women on Quests

Traditionally in quests, men are depicted as brave heroes or saviors who must endure peril or a series of tests of strength and character. Women are often either the reason behind the quest or the ones who need saving. For example, Homer's epic poem the *Odyssey* is a classic example of a traditional quest. It follows the fall of Troy and tells the story of Odysseus, who spends ten years trying to return to his wife, Penelope, in Ithaca. Along the way, he encounters many dangers, obstacles, and hardships before finally returning to his beloved. Sometimes, however, works involving a quest turn this tradition on its head.

One way to look at gender roles is through the lens of gender criticism. Gender criticism explores how an

Dorothy goes on a quest in order to end up back home where she started.

artistic work conveys ideas about men and women. It seeks to understand how creative pieces depict what is masculine and what is feminine. Gender criticism considers how characters portray each gender, how they interact, and how they are perceived. Gender criticism broadly analyzes works to consider how their depictions of what is masculine and feminine reflect society's notion of gender.

Similar to the *Odyssey*, *The Wonderful Wizard of Oz* recounts the story of a protagonist who is on a journey home. Like Odysseus, Dorothy faces challenges, danger, magical creatures, and lengthy travels to reach her goal. However, Dorothy's tale is different in that it challenges the stereotypes of gender within the quest theme. Dorothy deviates from classic gender stereotypes. By mustering courage in a strange land, she subverts the image of the classic damsel in distress who relies on a male for salvation. *The Wonderful Wizard of Oz* as a

Thesis

The thesis statement comes at the end of the first paragraph: "*The Wonderful Wizard of Oz* as a whole subverts some of the stereotypical assumptions about gender in quests by presenting female characters who are capable and brave and male characters who rely on female assistance and lack self-confidence and courage." The author will examine the actions of the characters in the book to support this idea.

whole subverts some of the stereotypical assumptions about gender in quests by presenting female characters who are capable and brave and male characters who rely on female assistance and lack self-confidence and courage.

Although Dorothy is a young farm girl, she has courage and intelligence and does not fall into the stereotype of needing a male character to save her. During her journey, she encounters many perilous situations that require bravery and rational thinking. As she sets out on the yellow brick road in a strange land, she begins her mission rationally and optimistically, without fear. She thinks ahead and packs food for her journey. Although she is a child who has been torn from her parental figures and everything familiar to her, she is polite and shows maturity when she meets strangers and eventually acts as her group's spokesperson.

A common thread in quest literature is overcoming seemingly unbeatable enemies in order to meet the end goal. Dorothy does this throughout the book with her

Argument One

The author begins arguing the thesis. The first argument is: "Although Dorothy is a young farm girl, she has courage and intelligence and does not fall into the stereotype of needing a male character to save her."

"You ought to be ashamed of yourself!"

Dorothy takes a leadership role in her group.

traveling companions' aid as they confront dangerous creatures and unfortunate mishaps. However, she ultimately defeats the Witch of the West by herself when she courageously stands up to her. It is Dorothy alone— not the brave young man of typical quest literature—

who vanquishes the powerful villain. Dorothy does this while the Tin Woodman and Scarecrow lay destroyed and helpless and the Cowardly Lion is caged. Dorothy doesn't need a male to win the battle for her. She is a self-sufficient heroine and is responsible for freeing the Winkies, Winged Monkeys, and other Oz-landers from the Witch's rule.

Unlike males in traditional quest tales, the Scarecrow, Woodman, and Lion are not brave and strong but rather turn to Dorothy, a girl, for help and guidance. When she meets a talking scarecrow, Dorothy is not afraid but instead devises a plan to help him down from his pole. When she hears his plight, she offers her help, saying, "If you will come with me I'll ask Oz to do all he can for you."[1] Instead of pairing up with a male character for her protection, Dorothy allows the Scarecrow to join her in hopes of helping him. The same is true with the Tin Woodman and Cowardly Lion. Dorothy saves the Woodman by oiling his joints, which frees him from captivity. While

Argument Two

The author gives another example, this time discussing male roles in the quest: "Unlike males in traditional quest tales, the Scarecrow, Woodman, and Lion are not brave and strong but rather turn to Dorothy, a girl, for help and guidance."

When the Wizard fails her, Dorothy rises to the occasion to save herself.

the Lion is held in the Witch's castle, Dorothy saves him from starvation by sneaking food to him during the night.

Males on a quest are often depicted as brave, confident, weapon-wielding characters. While the Scarecrow has smart ideas, the Tin Woodman shows compassion, and the Lion acts bravely, they do not recognize these qualities in themselves because they lack self-confidence. While the Tin Woodman does use his ax, it is primarily as a tool to cut branches and chop wood. Dorothy, on the other hand, possesses the true power in the group, wearing the magical Silver Shoes and commanding the Winged Monkeys with the Golden Cap. The male characters defer to Dorothy, who maturely fills the leadership role for the group. She believes in herself and does not need to ask the Wizard to change her character.

Ultimately, Dorothy looks to the wisest woman in the land to find the power to get home again. Unlike characters in typical quest literature, Dorothy does not reach her goal at the conclusion of the final epic battle, when she defeats the Wicked Witch. The Wizard, another male character, is unable to keep is promise. He is a con man, not an all-mighty being who has the power to grant the travelers their wishes. Instead, Dorothy has additional trials to endure and must travel greater distances to seek out the help of Glinda. Glinda, a woman, is more knowledgeable and in charge of the world than the male characters.

Argument Three

The author next argues: "Ultimately, Dorothy looks to the wisest woman in the land to find the power to get home again." The author raises some final points showing how gender in *The Wonderful Wizard of Oz* is different from traditional quest stories.

Throughout *The Wonderful Wizard of Oz,* Dorothy demonstrates she has intelligence, maturity, and the ability to survive in a strange land with dangerous creatures and evil adversaries. She is a strong female character who offers help, support, and guidance to her male travel companions even though she is a stranger in their land. Conversely, the Scarecrow, Tin Woodman, and Cowardly Lion, all male characters, lack self-confidence and knowledge. Dorothy proves that not every girl who sets out on a quest does so as the damsel in distress. Instead, she rises to the occasion and overturns classic notions that a strong character in a journey or quest setting must be male.

Conclusion

The final paragraph concludes the author's analysis and sums up the arguments that support the thesis.

Thinking Critically

Now it's your turn to assess the essay. Consider these questions:

1. The thesis statement proclaims the book goes against stereotypical assumptions about gender. Do you agree with this? Why or why not?

2. What additional arguments could the author have made that stem from the plot, characters, or additional elements that would have helped support the thesis?

3. The conclusion should restate the thesis and the main arguments of the essay. Does this conclusion do so effectively? Explain.

Other Approaches

There is never just one way to approach a work. You have read one way to think about the quest theme in *The Wonderful Wizard of Oz*, considering the role of gender. Other analyses could consider archetypes in the book or the book's relationship to US history.

Archetypes of Growing Up

Archetypal criticism seeks to relate characters to other well-known characters, symbols, or ideas. One characteristic of the hero's journey archetype is an event that helps the hero grow up. At the beginning of the story, when Dorothy is in Kansas, everything around her is gray, from the prairie to the house. The only thing that brings Dorothy happiness is her dog, Toto. But by the end of the story, Dorothy is thrilled to finally return home to the drab Kansas prairie and her aunt and uncle. A possible thesis for an essay that examines these ideas might be: Through her quest in Oz, Dorothy emerges at the end of the story as a more mature character with a greater appreciation for her family and home.

Kansas History

Historical criticism looks at the historical and social circumstances of the time when a work was created. It then analyzes how the work was influenced by the time in which it was produced.

When *The Wonderful Wizard of Oz* was written, Kansas was suffering from terrible droughts and poverty. Dorothy leaves a dull gray existence and arrives in Oz, where she encounters a bright world with Silver Shoes, the Emerald City, and other items that represent wealth. One might argue that L. Frank Baum was making a statement about the plight of Midwestern farmers at the time of the book's writing. A possible thesis statement that views Dorothy's quest through a historical lens might be: *The Wonderful Wizard of Oz* presents a quest story that mirrors the quest of the Everyman to improve his fortune during economic hardship.

4

AN OVERVIEW OF

The Hunger Games

*T*he 2008 young adult book *The Hunger Games*, by Suzanne Collins, takes place in a dystopian, postapocalyptic nation in North America called Panem. The continent is ruled from the wealthy Capitol district. Twelve surrounding districts are poor and oppressed under the fascist control of the Capitol's President Snow.

The Reaping

Sixteen-year-old Katniss Everdeen lives with her mother and younger sister, Primrose, in the coal-mining District 12. As the story opens, Katniss meets her male friend Gale outside her district's fence. The two teens

Katniss Everdeen's quest is to survive and save her family.

hunt for meat to supplement their meager rations. Before Katniss's father died, he taught her to use a bow.

Katniss and Gale talk about the Hunger Games reaping ceremony that will take place later in the day. Following a failed rebellion against the Capitol years before, the Hunger Games were enacted. Every year, one girl and one boy from each district are chosen by a lottery system to act as tributes in the annual Hunger Games. The 24 tributes must participate in a fight-to-the-death battle in an outdoor arena until only one victor remains. The games are controlled by the Capitol and televised throughout all districts. The games remind the districts of the power of the Capitol and discourage future rebellions.

At the reaping, Effie Trinket, a bright and bubbly citizen of the Capitol, draws names from large glass bowls. From the podium before the crowd, she says her usual slogan, "Happy Hunger Games! And may the odds be *ever* in your favor!"[1] Katniss's younger sister, Prim's, name is drawn. Desperate to save her sister, Katniss volunteers to take her place, thus beginning her quest. Peeta Mellark, a boy Katniss knows from school, is chosen as the male tribute. Peeta once gave Katniss bread from his family's bakery when the Everdeen

Katniss's quest begins when she volunteers as tribute in her sister's place.

family was on the verge of starvation. She remembers his kindness to her. The two are taken by train to the Capitol and meet their mentor, Haymitch Abernathy, a former victor from District 12. Katniss is unimpressed by Haymitch, who spends most of his time drinking.

To the Capitol

Television personality Caesar Flickerman interviews the 24 tributes after they've had fashion makeovers from stylists assigned to them. Haymitch and Effie encourage Katniss and Peeta to be appealing to the viewing audience so sponsors will send them medicine and food during the games. While being interviewed, Peeta admits to falling in love with Katniss, which angers her. Katniss dislikes the media exposure.

The tributes train together, and Haymitch instructs the pair to watch the other tributes for strengths and weaknesses. Coming out of training, Katniss earns a high score, something that will attract sponsors. She scares and impresses the judges when she shoots an arrow directly at them, splitting the apple in the mouth of the roast pig they were about to eat.

When the first day of the Hunger Games arrives, Katniss's stylist, Cinna, remains with her. Although Cinna is from the Capitol, he does not buy into the sensationalism of the Games, and Katniss trusts and respects him. "Remember what Haymitch said," he reminds her. "Run, find water. The rest will follow."[2]

The Games

The tributes are lifted through underground tubes into the arena. Ahead of her, Katniss sees a large Cornucopia stocked with supplies and weapons. Instead of running toward the Cornucopia, Katniss scoops up a bright orange backpack near her and flees. Behind her, tributes slaughter each other and fight for provisions. She later inventories her backpack and finds some crucial supplies.

Katniss's skill with a bow is key to her survival.

That night, Katniss realizes 11 of her opponents have already fallen. Peeta is still alive. Before dawn the following morning, she sees a wall of fire moving toward her. She flees, but her leg receives a bad burn. She takes refuge that night in a tree. She sees Rue, the 12-year-old female tribute from District 11, the agricultural district, hiding in the treetops as well. As a group of opponents forms under Katniss's tree, Rue points to a nest of tracker jacker wasps near Katniss. Katniss cuts down the nest. When it hits the ground, the others run from the deadly stings of the genetically engineered insects. Two members of the group die from stings, and Katniss sees one of the victims has a bow and arrows. As she grabs the bow, Peeta arrives. He tells her to run and stops Cato, a strong and threatening tribute, as she makes her escape.

Katniss's feelings for Peeta are confused for much of the book.

An Alliance

Katniss finds a stream for water and uses her bow to kill a rabbit and a wild bird. She discovers Rue is watching her. She proposes an alliance with the girl. The young girl reminds Katniss of Prim.

That night, Rue explains the most dangerous group of competitors has all the food and supplies at the Cornucopia. The two girls begin devising their first offensive plan, to blow up the supplies. Rue lights fires as a diversion while Katniss sets off a mine, which blows up the food and supplies. Then Katniss goes in search of Rue and finds another tribute stabbing her with a spear. Katniss kills the tribute and then holds Rue and sings to her as she dies. Her hatred of the Capitol is renewed.

Katniss hears a voice announce from overhead that there is a rule change. Two tributes can win as long as they are from the same district. Peeta's confession of love has swayed the audience, which is now rooting for the star-crossed lovers. Realizing both she and Peeta can win together, she searches for him.

Katniss finds Peeta by a stream. He has camouflaged himself into the leaves and mud and is injured badly. Katniss helps him to a cave, where they take refuge. Peeta's condition worsens, and, thinking he might die, Katniss kisses him. Immediately she receives a pot of broth as a gift from Haymitch. She decides playing up the supposed romance might help them. Another announcement says the remaining tributes are all in need of something, and those items will be provided at the Cornucopia. Katniss knows Peeta will die without medicine, but Peeta thinks it's a suicide mission for her to go and tells her not to. When Peeta falls asleep, Katniss leaves. Katniss makes it back to Peeta with the medicine, and the two spend the next few days in the cave while it rains nonstop. Katniss plays up the star-crossed lover ruse in order to get more sponsor gifts, but it seems a real romance is starting.

Victory

Peeta and Katniss finally emerge from the cave. Peeta gathers berries while Katniss hunts. He doesn't realize the berries are poisonous. Katniss keeps the berries anyway so she might be able to trick Cato into eating them. Cato is the only other tribute left.

As they make their way toward the Cornucopia for water, Cato runs past them. Muttations—large, mutant, wolflike mutts—are on his heels. Katniss and Peeta pull themselves up onto the Cornucopia, but Cato attacks once they are on top. They push him over the edge. The animals attack him, and Katniss shoots him.

Peeta and Katniss believe they've won. However, a voice announces, "The earlier revision has been revoked. Closer examination of the rule book has disclosed that only one winner may be allowed. Good luck and may the odds be ever in your favor."[3]

Refusing to kill Peeta, Katniss pours the poisonous berries into their hands. They agree to eat them on the count of three. Just as the berries enter their mouths, shouts from above stop them. Both Katniss and Peeta are announced as the winners.

It is clear when Katniss returns victorious that President Snow is her enemy.

What Awaits Back Home

Katniss and Peeta return to the Capitol Training Center. Haymitch tells Katniss the Capitol is not pleased with her defiance. Under his instruction, she convinces everyone in her final interview that she was so in love with Peeta she couldn't bear the thought of living without him. Peeta realizes that Katniss feigned affection in order to secure sympathy and sponsor gifts. He is heartbroken.

The two have no choice but to pretend they are in love until the cameras are gone. Katniss is now considered a political enemy for her public defiance against the Capitol. She has conflicted feelings for Peeta and Gale as she returns home.

5

The Flawed Mentor

*M*entors are common archetypes in literature, film, and art. A reader or a viewer can readily relate to these common symbolic individuals or themes. Swiss psychiatrist Carl Jung first made famous the idea of a collective unconscious that is shared among people. This shared unconscious causes them to recognize a similar cast of characters and situations. American scholar Joseph Campbell later expanded Jung's ideas, recognizing similar narrative patterns in literary works around the world. Archetypal criticism evaluates a book, film, or other piece of art through an archetype.

Some of the more familiar archetypal characters are the hero, the trickster, the warrior, the underdog,

As is common for many heroes, Katniss must complete her quest without her mentors.

the mother, and the father. The list of archetypes is wide ranging and also includes such characters as the herald, the mentor, the wise old sage or magician, the goddess, and the Christ figure. Common nonliving archetypes are birth, death, rebirth, forbidden fruit, harvest, fear, or loss. The quest or journey is also a very popular archetype. The reader or the viewer connects with these people or ideas and shares emotionally in their experiences.

Archetypes are an integral part of journey and quest literature. They help motivate and guide the protagonist, they assist the protagonist in discovering things about themselves, and they are often the obstacles or dangers that the quester must overcome. The modern-day quest story *The Hunger Games* is no exception. The book features heroes, heralds, mother and father figures, star-crossed lovers, magicians, and more. The mentor is typically very wise and older than the hero. He or she teaches and guides the hero and in some instances provides gifts or tools that allow the protagonist to continue the journey. However, the archetype of mentor breaks the usual pattern in *The Hunger Games*. Unlike well-known mentors such as Yoda in *Star Wars* or Professor Dumbledore in the Harry Potter series,

Haymitch Abernathy is a flawed character who is difficult to trust and has questionable abilities. Haymitch is an unreliable mentor but ultimately has a positive effect on Katniss's quest despite his flaws.

Thesis Statement

Here, the author states the thesis: "Haymitch is an unreliable mentor but ultimately has a positive effect on Katniss's quest despite his flaws." The author will provide arguments backing up this statement.

Haymitch's alcoholism greatly calls into question his moral compass and his ability to mentor Katniss on her quest. At the Hunger Games reaping, Haymitch is introduced on stage. He is so drunk his speech is unintelligible, and he falls into his chair. When Katniss and Peeta accompany him and Effie on the train to the Capitol, Haymitch arrives for supper drunk and soon vomits. When Peeta and Katniss laugh off the behavior as typical for Haymitch, Effie admonishes both of them, reminding them, "You know your mentor is your lifeline to the world

Argument One

The author makes the first argument defending the thesis: "Haymitch's alcoholism greatly calls into question his moral compass and his ability to mentor Katniss on her quest." The author begins by explaining why Haymitch seems unreliable.

Haymitch's drinking problem and emotional issues make it difficult for Katniss to understand and trust him.

in these Games. The one who advises you, lines up your sponsors, and dictates the presentation of any gifts. Haymitch can well be the difference between your life and your death!"[1] When the train reaches the Capitol, Haymitch disappears until after the opening ceremonies, leaving Katniss to face her styling team and her first public appearance by herself. Katniss assumes he's drunk.

Katniss and Peeta must prod Haymitch into taking his duties seriously. They take him to his room after he vomits on the train. When Haymitch's first advice to the pair is, "Stay alive," Peeta knocks the drink out of Haymitch's hand.[2] Haymitch punches Peeta, and Katniss stabs at Haymitch, barely missing his hand. It is only after they lash out that Haymitch takes any interest in acting as a mentor, saying, "Well, what's this? . . . Did I actually get a pair of fighters this year?"[3] Haymitch refuses to stop drinking, only promising to "stay sober enough to help" if Katniss follows all his instructions.[4] After the opening ceremonies, Effie steps up and tries to secure sponsorships to help Katniss and Peeta get through the games. However, Haymitch needs to be present to formalize the deals.

Haymitch finally turns his behavior around and begins helping and advising Katniss and Peeta, but his relationship with Katniss is not one of mutual respect. Typically, a protagonist is grateful for his or her mentor's advice when proceeding on a quest. But Katniss begrudgingly takes Haymitch's advice. She resents his advice to play up a relationship with Peeta for the cameras. She is annoyed throughout her discussions with Haymitch about her training. Her difficulty

Argument Two

The author provides more evidence about Haymitch and Katniss's relationship: "Haymitch finally turns his behavior around and begins helping and advising Katniss and Peeta, but his relationship with Katniss is not one of mutual respect."

working with Haymitch comes close to jeopardizing her television interview. She is unable to effectively practice for her appearance with Haymitch. His harsh feedback wounds her when he says she's "got about as much charm as a dead slug."[5] Instead she relies on her stylist Cinna's advice to get her through. When Peeta reveals that Haymitch helped him plan his public declaration of love, Katniss believes Haymitch has chosen to help Peeta survive over her.

Argument Three

The author examines the effect Haymitch's mentoring has had on Katniss's quest: "As Katniss enters the Hunger Games without her mentor, it is unclear whether Haymitch has helped her much."

As Katniss enters the Hunger Games without her mentor, it is unclear whether Haymitch has helped her much. Despite all of Haymitch's training advice, Katniss's high score is tied to her own decision to shoot an arrow toward the judges. Katniss's success on television is because of her own personality and Cinna's coaching much more than Haymitch's prodding. Although Haymitch sends her sponsor gifts throughout the game, the gifts come at a price. She must act in love with Peeta in order to receive

By the book's end, Katniss has more trust and faith in her mentor.

Haymitch's rewards. Katniss must complete her quest using her own talents and resources.

Although he is not a reliable mentor, Haymitch still assists in Katniss's quest. During the Hunger Games, Katniss realizes Haymitch is using the sponsor gifts as subtle clues. Katniss believes Haymitch has deserted her when she nearly dies from lack of water. She soon realizes that by not sending water when she asked for it, he was giving her a clue that water was nearby. Katniss

Argument Four

The author assesses Haymitch's contributions to Katniss's quest: "Although he is not a reliable mentor, Haymitch still assists in Katniss's quest."

also realizes Haymitch is rewarding her for acting in love because he believes it will help her get sympathy from sponsors, thus helping her survive.

Haymitch's drunkenness and harsh feedback do not fit the traditional mold of mentor. As the protagonist of the quest, Katniss must rely on other companions and herself to fill the holes his clumsy mentorship leaves. But Haymitch's gifts come in time to save Katniss and Peeta's lives. And when Katniss returns from the Games victorious, it is clear Haymitch is firmly on her side going forward to the second book in the trilogy. Katniss has completed her first quest, and while doing so, gained a mentor who will become more valuable as her story continues.

Conclusion

In the final paragraph, the author analyzes the final effect of Haymitch's mentorship on Katniss's quest and considers their relationship moving forward in the trilogy.

Thinking Critically

Now it's your turn to assess the essay. Consider these questions:

1. *The Hunger Games* takes place in a dystopian society. Do you think that setting affects the archetypes and their behaviors? If so, how?

2. Consider the arguments the author has made about Katniss's mentor. What additional evidence from the book could support the author's claims? Is there evidence that contradicts the author's thesis?

3. *The Hunger Games* includes many archetypes typical of a quest story. In what ways is *The Hunger Games* a classic quest? In what ways is it unique or different?

Other Approaches

Archetypal criticism offers a variety of approaches to apply to a chosen work of literature. In 1949, Joseph Campbell wrote *The Hero with a Thousand Faces*, which has become an authoritative source on the hero's journey throughout mythology. Campbell mostly focuses on the masculine journey. Females are mainly mothers, lovers, witches, temptresses, or goddesses. Thinking of the traditional hero in terms of being male, another approach to critiquing *The Hunger Games* through the lens of archetypal theory might be to explore the inherent differences between a man's quest and a woman's quest. A different approach to archetypes in the *Hunger Games* might instead examine Effie's role as the herald.

The Female Hero in Quest Literature

One common stereotype in quest literature is that the hero is traditionally male. Are there differences that occur if the hero is female rather than male? How is the female portrayed in a heroic journey? In typical female quests, the woman pits intelligence against her enemies rather than her strength. A thesis exploring this idea could be: *The Hunger Games* is an atypical quest story because it requires the female hero to have physical strength, combat abilities, and survival skills.

Effie as Herald

The herald archetype serves the purpose of signaling change and inviting the character to answer the call to adventure. Heralds impart important information about the upcoming journey. They often set things in motion by explaining the rules or decreeing what must be done. The herald is an important messenger to both the protagonist and the audience. Effie, however, is not a simple herald, but an explicit supporter of the Capitol and the Hunger Games. A thesis about the effect of Effie's bias could be: Effie's favorable bias toward the Capitol and the Hunger Games affects her role as herald, starting Katniss's quest on the wrong foot from the very beginning.

6

AN OVERVIEW OF THE
Lord of the Rings Trilogy

*T*he Lord of the Rings film trilogy depicts the three-volume epic high fantasy novel by J. R. R. Tolkien. The three films are *The Fellowship of the Ring* (2001), *The Two Towers* (2002), and *The Return of the King* (2003). Tolkien's world is populated by elves, wizards, dwarves, humans, and hobbits (smaller relatives of humans), among other creatures of legend. The story begins with a prehistory of the One Ring. The Dark Lord Sauron forged it in the fires of Mount Doom of Mordor as the ultimate weapon to assist him in conquering Middle-earth. During battle, Isildur, a prince of the human kingdom of Gondor, takes the ring. When presented with the opportunity to destroy the evil ring,

At the heart of the Lord of the Rings trilogy is the quest to destroy the One Ring.

he choses instead to keep it, because, as the voiceover explains, "The hearts of men are easily corrupted."[1] Isildur loses the ring, and eventually the creature Sméagol finds it and takes it to his cave. Later the hobbit Bilbo Baggins finds the ring and keeps it.

Leaving the Shire

The scene cuts to the peaceful Shire, home of the hobbits, where many years later Bilbo is preparing for his 111th birthday party. The wizard Gandalf the Grey arrives. Unbeknownst to Bilbo's nephew Frodo, Bilbo is planning to leave the Shire and will leave his possessions to the younger hobbit. During his birthday speech, Bilbo slips on the ring, which makes him invisible, and he rushes back to his house to grab his belongings and leave. Gandalf is waiting for him. At Gandalf's insistence, Bilbo also leaves the ring.

Gandalf has discovered the ring is Sauron's, and evil undead riders known as the ringwraiths are closing in on the Shire and Bilbo's house. Gandalf tells Frodo the ring must leave the Shire, or all hobbits living there will be in danger. Frodo offers it to Gandalf, but the wizard replies, "Don't tempt me, Frodo! . . . I would use this ring from a desire to do good. But through me, it would wield a power too great and terrible to imagine."[2] Gandalf sends Frodo with his friend Sam to the town of Bree, where they are to meet up after Gandalf consults with the leader of the wizards.

The two hobbits bump into their friends Merry and Pippin. Soon the foursome is running to escape the ringwraiths. They make it to Bree, but Gandalf is not there. While at the Prancing Pony, Frodo falls and the ring slips onto his finger, making him invisible. Wearing the ring alerts the ringwraiths to the hobbits' location. With the help of a mysterious human called Strider, the hobbits escape the ringwraiths.

The hobbits and Strider make for Rivendell, home of the elves. However, along the way, a ringwraith stabs Frodo. Arwen, an elvish princess, shows up and flees with Frodo on horseback to Rivendell, outrunning the ringwraiths.

A Fellowship Is Formed

When Frodo awakens he is in Rivendell, where Arwen's father, Elrond, has healed him. Gandalf meets up with Frodo at last. The wizard had been imprisoned by his mentor, Saruman, who wants the ring for himself. Gandalf and Elrond decide the ring must be destroyed.

Elrond convenes a meeting, calling the races of Middle-earth together. The council decides someone must travel to Mordor and throw the ring into the fires of Mount Doom. Frodo volunteers. Others step forward to accompany him, and the Fellowship of the Ring is formed. It consists of Gandalf, the man Boromir of Gondor, Legolas the elf, Gimli the dwarf, the four hobbits, and Strider, whose real name is Aragorn.

The fellowship endures a number of trials and mishaps as they make their way through Middle-earth. In the mines of Moria, the party flees an army of inhuman creatures called orcs and loses Gandalf to a Balrog, a demonic creature from the underworld. The others press on, making their way to another settlement of elves and Galadriel, the Lady of the Woods. Frodo speaks with Galadriel, who tells him he alone must accomplish the task, or no one will. The next morning they depart by river, but when they dock on land, the party is attacked by Uruk-hai, a large and powerful type of orc under Saruman's command. Boromir is killed, and Merry and Pippin are taken prisoner. Frodo is forlorn and departs in a boat. Sam insists on coming along, and the two travel on toward Mordor.

The Fellowship of the Ring has nine members including men, hobbits, an elf, a dwarf, and a wizard.

The Two Towers

At the beginning of the second film, it is revealed that Gandalf did not die. He actually killed the Balrog as the two fell into a chasm.

Frodo and Sam feel as if they're going in circles. The ring, which Frodo wears on a chain around his neck, seems to be affecting him. It tempts him to put it on, which would alert the ringwraiths to their location. They come across Gollum, the creature once known as Sméagol who owned the ring. After a fight, the hobbits overcome Gollum. He agrees to lead them to Mordor.

Aragorn, Legolas, and Gimli cross paths with the human riders of Rohan. Saruman has cast a spell on the king of Rohan. The group attacks the Uruk-hai, and Merry and Pippin are able to escape alone into an enchanted forest. Aragorn tracks footprints into the woods, where they meet Gandalf, who has been transformed into Gandalf the White. Gandalf informs them that war has come to Rohan. Together the four travel to the castle of King Théoden, where Gandalf releases him from the spell. The people evacuate to the fort at Helm's Deep. There they fight a ferocious battle. Against all odds, they are victorious. However, it is evident the battle for Middle-earth has just begun.

Meanwhile, Frodo, Sam, and Gollum arrive at the gates of Mordor but realize they will have to use a back entrance in order to enter undetected. Sam can see the ring is starting to take over Frodo, while Frodo starts feeling compassion for Gollum. It becomes apparent that Gollum has a split personality. His good side, Sméagol, wants to help the hobbits, while Gollum, his evil half, plots to kill the hobbits and take back the ring.

The Return of the King

Merry and Pippin are reunited with Gandalf, Aragorn, and Legolas. Gandalf and Pippin leave for Minas Tirith, a city in Gondor, to warn that Sauron is planning to attack. In Minas Tirith, Lord Denethor, Boromir's father, is angered by the return of Aragorn, who is the

Gollum's two personalities war inside his head.

proper heir to the throne of Gondor. He refuses to listen to Gandalf's warnings about the upcoming battle.

Frodo and Sam continue on with Gollum. The ring is taking hold of Frodo and clouding his judgment. Frodo becomes suspicious of Sam when he offers to carry the ring. Frodo decides to go on with just Gollum.

Meanwhile, Aragorn enlists the help of an army of ghost warriors who dwell in a mountain cave. He asserts himself as the king of Gondor. The ghosts are bound to honor the king and follow his orders. In Minas Tirith, Gandalf takes over command of the castle and fortress when Denethor orders his men to abandon their posts. The riders of Rohan arrive to help.

Gollum leads Frodo into the cave of Shelob, a giant spider. Gollum then disappears, intending to steal the ring back once the spider has killed Frodo. But Sam arrives and fights Gollum. He rescues Frodo after orcs take off with his spiderweb-wrapped body. The two set off toward Mount Doom together.

At Minas Tirith, Sauron's army arrives on the battlefield. The riders of Rohan are struggling. King Théoden is killed. Aragorn arrives with his army of ghost warriors, who quickly kill any remaining orcs.

As Frodo and Sam make their way through Mordor, they run out of water. The ring weighs heavily on Frodo. Both accept that they will not last for a return journey. When they finally reach Mount Doom, Frodo is unable to drop the ring into the fire. "The ring is mine," he declares and puts it on.[3] Sam watches as his friend falls completely under the power of the ring.

Suddenly Gollum attacks Frodo, biting off his finger to get the ring. The two struggle, and Gollum and the ring fall over the edge of a cliff into the lava below. The ring disintegrates. Instantly the eye of Sauron burns out, and the tower of Mordor begins collapsing. Frodo and Sam make it to a giant boulder as the mountain erupts,

Frodo and Sam complete the last leg of the quest together.

spewing lava. Accepting their coming deaths, the two
are suddenly rescued by giant eagles.

Frodo awakens back in Rivendell with his friends at
his side. Gandalf crowns Aragorn as king of Gondor.

Frodo and Sam return to the Shire, where Sam
marries Rosie, the girl he has secretly loved for some
time. Frodo writes of his experiences in a book he calls
The Lord of the Rings. Four years after he was wounded by
the ringwraith, he still struggles with all he has endured
as the ring-bearer. He joins Gandalf as they sail away
with the elves into the Undying Lands of eternal life.
Sam is heartbroken to see him go. "We set out to save
the Shire, Sam. And it has been saved," Frodo reassures
his best friend.[4] He embraces Sam, Merry, and Pippin
and then sets sail with Gandalf.

A Religious Journey

*A*n allegory is a literary device that conveys a hidden meaning within a piece of literature or artwork. It provides two levels of meaning within the work. At the surface is the basic story. This includes the characters and plot as they are written. However, there is also an allegorical meaning to the piece, a deeper meaning below the surface. This is achieved through the use of symbolic figures, actions, imagery, or events that create a moral, spiritual, or political meaning. Religious allegory gives a piece a layer of symbolic meaning through religious themes or ideas.

The Lord of the Rings trilogy tells the tale of Frodo Baggins, a humble hobbit who is called to a difficult and dangerous quest to save the inhabitants of

POWER CAN BE HELD
IN THE SMALLEST OF THINGS

THE TRILOGY BEGINS DECEMBER 2001

The One Ring's evil power can be understood through
religious allegory.

Middle-earth from destruction by the evil Dark Lord Sauron. A faithful group of companions helps him realize his goal. Ready to defend him to the death, this fellowship follows him into the unknown because they believe in his mission and view him as the only one who can defeat darkness by destroying the ring.

Frodo's quest in the Lord of the Rings trilogy serves as a Christian allegory about the salvation of mankind through the journey of a Christlike character.

Frodo and Jesus Christ are both unlikely saviors on a quest to save humanity. Much like Jesus Christ, whose story of birth, life, and crucifixion on a cross is told in the New Testament books of the Bible, Frodo is born of humble birth. Frodo is a peaceful hobbit who has never ventured out of the

Thesis

The author presents the thesis, setting up the idea of Frodo's quest as a religious allegory: "Frodo's quest in the Lord of the Rings trilogy serves as a Christian allegory about the salvation of mankind through the journey of a Christlike character."

Argument One

The author makes the first argument, introducing the two figures who will be compared: "Frodo and Jesus Christ are both unlikely saviors on a quest to save humanity."

Shire, and Jesus is also born to commoners and grows up leading a simple life. Neither is born to great wealth or status. Instead of training for battle as a knight or great warrior would, Frodo grows up learning how to tend a garden, and Jesus, a simple carpenter, eventually spends his days serving others. In Tolkien's world, hobbits are known to be creatures of comfort who don't journey far from the Shire. They are content with predictability and simplicity. Although Jesus grew up knowing he would one day tell others about God, his ambitions were simple and nonmaterialistic.

Both Frodo and Jesus's quests involve a great burden: only they can save humanity from the rule of darkness, represented by Sauron in the Lord of the Rings series and Satan in the Bible. Jesus was born as a man with the godly powers of his father. He has the ability to simply turn away from the pain and suffering he knows is in his future. Frodo could simply end his mission and turn from the perils of his quest, saving

Argument Two

The author compares the challenges Frodo and Jesus both face: "Both Frodo and Jesus's quests involve a great burden: only they can save humanity from the rule of darkness, represented by Sauron in the Lord of the Rings series and Satan in the Bible."

Jesus and Frodo both continue their quests through pain and suffering.

himself instead of continuing on his dangerous journey. But the fate of all Middle-earth is in Frodo's hands. Frodo offers the ring to Gandalf and Galadriel, but they tell him he alone must bear the burden of carrying the ring to Mount Doom. Jesus knows no other can die to save mankind from sin and darkness. Both ask to give up their burdens but ultimately carry on. The night he is taken into custody before being crucified, Jesus prays to God, asking, "Father, if you are willing, take this cup from me; yet not my will, but yours be done."[1] He asks God to spare him the pain and suffering, but he knows it is ultimately God's decision.

During their quests, both Frodo and Jesus endure physical pain and pay the ultimate sacrifice. While on his mission to save Middle-earth, Frodo is stabbed by a ringwraith and bitten by a giant spider.

Argument Three

The author compares another similarity between Frodo and Jesus: "During their quests, both Frodo and Jesus endure physical pain and pay the ultimate sacrifice."

He endures hunger and exhaustion, has his finger bitten off by Gollum, and ultimately is so scarred by his experience that he leaves the human world and sails off into the Undying Lands with Gandalf. During his crucifixion, Jesus is whipped, beaten, crowned with a ring of thorns, and finally nailed to a cross, where he dies. Just before his death, Jesus says that he is thirsty. Similarly, as Frodo and Sam ascend Mount Doom, Frodo attempts to get some water, but the two have run out. The scene parallels Jesus's thirst in his final hours.

Frodo's journey through Mordor and salvation by the giant eagle is symbolic of Jesus's death and descent into hell before rising back up on the third day following his death. Mordor is a blackened wasteland of evil with

Frodo and Jesus both have companions who care deeply for them.

a fiery volcano at its heart. Upon dropping the ring in the fire and destroying it—thereby overcoming evil and saving Middle-earth from Sauron—Frodo finds himself in a fiery hell. Just before the lava destroys him, a giant bird saves him. Similarly, after Jesus dies on the cross, his soul descends into the fiery inferno of hell. He spends three days paying for the sins of mankind. He then rises up and leaves behind the death and destruction of hell. Both Frodo and Jesus are reunited with their traveling companions, Frodo with his fellowship and Jesus with his faithful disciples. Both characters spend time with their friends before they are taken off to an immortal life. Jesus ascends into heaven, and Frodo sets sail for the Undying Lands. Just as Sam is heartbroken to see Frodo leave, so too is Jesus's closest ally, the Apostle John. But both Frodo and Jesus reassure Sam and John that their work is now done and the quest complete.

Another parallel is that both Frodo and Jesus are tempted by evil forces as they continue their quests. Frodo is often tempted to use the ring, which embodies the power of Sauron. The ring makes its wearer invisible, an invaluable tool for hiding from enemies. Yet it draws the ringwraiths to it, increasing its wearer's peril. In time, the ring will turn its wearer into another ringwraith, so choosing to use the ring leads eventually to its wearer's death. Jesus was also tempted by Satan prior to his crucifixion. In the New Testament book of Luke, Jesus wanders in the desert for 40 days and does not eat. Satan appears and tempts him, telling him he should merely use his power to change some rocks into bread. Later, as Jesus hangs upon the cross, he is taunted by passersby who yell, "Come down from

Argument Four

The author finds more evidence linking the two figures: "Another parallel is that both Frodo and Jesus are tempted by evil forces as they continue their quests."

the cross, if you are the Son of God!"[2] However, unlike Jesus, Frodo sometimes gives into temptation and puts on the ring. Indeed, at the climax of the story, Frodo does not give up the ring willingly. The ring is destroyed when Gollum bites it from Frodo's finger and falls into the chasm. Frodo has many similarities to Jesus but he is more flawed.

Argument Five

The author considers other aspects of the story that support the thesis: "Apart from Frodo and Jesus, there are other allusions in the Lord of the Rings that point toward a deeper symbolic representation of the Bible."

Apart from Frodo and Jesus, there are other allusions in the Lord of the Rings that point toward a deeper symbolic representation of the Bible. The fellowship represents Christians from vastly different backgrounds, races, and cultures coming together to unite against evil. Frodo's companions are men, elves, and dwarves, and Jesus's disciples also come from diverse backgrounds. The presence of magic in the Lord of the Rings symbolizes the miracles Jesus and his disciples performed. In addition, the character of Galadriel, the Lady of Lothlorien, can be compared to the Virgin Mary as Catholics see her. Both are represented as caring,

The character of Galadriel can also be understood through religious allegory.

nurturing female figures, bathed in light and beauty. Mary is beloved by Catholics and often referred to as "Our Lady," and Galadriel is revered by the inhabitants of Middle-earth. Upon meeting her, Sam refers to her as "the Lady."[3] As Catholics pray to Mary for help, guidance, and blessings, so does the fellowship turn to Galadriel for guidance and aid. Galadriel reassures Frodo and his friends. She also gives each of them a gift, including a phial to Frodo, which is a light "in dark places, when all other lights go out."[4] Comparable to the light of Mary's love and guidance, which offers Catholics hope, Galadriel's light helps save Frodo when he and Sam are in the lair of Shelob.

While the Lord of the Rings is, on the surface, a story of a young hobbit and his fellows who go on a quest to save their land from complete destruction, under the surface it also serves as a religious allegory to the journey of Jesus, who saves mankind from eternal damnation. Tolkien's use of biblical-type characters and scenarios in the Lord of the Rings presents the Jesus figure as a reimagined character who also rises from a humble life to endure a perilous quest to save mankind from doom and despair, just as Jesus did by dying on the cross to redeem mankind from sin. As Galadriel's voiceover at the beginning of *The Fellowship of the Ring* explains, "The time will soon come when hobbits will shape the fortunes of all."[5] Instead of choosing a graceful and wise elf, a battle-hardened dwarf, or a noble knight to save Middle-earth, Tolkien assigned the task to a modest and ordinary hobbit, just as a humble man saves mankind in the Bible.

Conclusion
The author wraps up the arguments and ties them back to the original thesis.

Thinking Critically

Now it's your turn to assess the essay. Consider these questions:

1. The thesis statement asserts that Frodo's quest in the Lord of the Rings is a religious allegory to the Christ story in the Bible. Do you agree with this? Can you think of any arguments to refute this?

2. What was the most interesting argument made? What other plot or character elements could be used to support the thesis?

3. Can you think of any other allegories that might exist in *The Lord of the Rings?* What evidence from the film would you use to support those allegories?

Other Approaches

What you have read is one possible way to critique the theme of the quest in the Lord of the Rings. Other writers and experts have approached it in different ways. Following are two other approaches one might take in viewing the quest in the film trilogy.

Aragorn's Quest for Redemption

In *The Fellowship of the Ring*, it is revealed that Aragorn is the descendant of Isildur, the king of Gondor who is responsible for not destroying the One Ring when he had the chance. His greed therefore allowed the evil of Sauron to endure. In the subsequent films, it becomes evident that Aragorn is the rightful heir of Gondor, but he has refused to claim the throne because of the guilt he feels over his ancestor's failure. Many have argued the Lord of the Rings trilogy is the journey of Aragorn's redemption. By the end of *The Return of the King*, having defeated Sauron's armies, Aragorn assumes his rightful place as the king of Gondor. The thesis for a critique that examines the quest of Aragorn might be: As Aragorn helps Frodo in the quest to destroy the One Ring and bring down Sauron, he is also on a quest for redemption from the mistakes of his ancestor.

Arguing against Religious Allegory

Some writers and experts have argued against a biblical allegory in the Lord of the Rings. They argue that, unlike Christ, Frodo ultimately fails in his quest when he refuses to throw the ring into the fires of Mount Doom. Furthermore, some argue that after Frodo returns to the Shire, he is so saddened and plagued by guilt that he has no choice but to leave his friends and family and be taken away to the Undying Lands. It seems that Frodo has not found forgiveness, nor can anyone absolve him of his sins. A thesis statement for such a critique might be: The character of Frodo in the Lord of the Rings does not represent Christ in an allegory that parallels the Bible because unlike Christ, Frodo fails in his quest and succumbs to evil.

AN OVERVIEW OF

Sir Gawain and the Green Knight

An unknown author in England wrote the poem *Sir Gawain and the Green Knight* between approximately 1375 and 1400 CE. The *Gawain* poet left behind only three other poems. However, his sophisticated writing and handling of the narrative are remarkable and point to him being an educated man. The poem is an Arthurian romance that tells the story of a noble knight who undergoes a quest in order to prove himself and retain his honor. This is a common theme throughout medieval literature, as is seen in writings about the legendary King Arthur and his court at Camelot.

King Arthur and his knights are traditional characters in quest stories.

The Beheading Game

The poem opens on a New Year's feast in Camelot. King Arthur and his Knights of the Round Table are celebrating with the lords and ladies of the court. An unexpected and unknown visitor arrives. He is dressed all in green and riding a green horse. Known only as the Green Knight, the gigantic visitor challenges King Arthur or any other brave man to a game. He will allow his opponent the chance to strike him with his own ax. However, one year and one day later, the challenger must find him to receive a blow in return. As a reward, the challenger will be able to keep the Green Knight's mighty ax, which is:

> *A wicked piece of work in words to expound:*
> *The head on its haft was an ell [roughly a yard] long;*
> *The spike of green steel, resplendent with gold;*
> *The blade burnished bright, with a broad edge,*
> *As well shaped to shear as a sharp razor[1]*

When Arthur hesitates, Sir Gawain, his youngest knight and nephew, leaps up to accept the challenge himself. He takes up the giant's ax and takes off the Green Knight's head with one blow. But instead of falling to his death, the Green Knight arises and picks up

Magical events, such as a beheaded knight riding off with his head, are common in quest stories.

his head. He remounts his horse and holds up his head. "Sir Gawain, forget not to go as agreed," it states.[2] The Green Knight rides off, holding his head, and Gawain and King Arthur hang the ax above the dais as a trophy for all the knights to admire.

Setting Out to Honor the Pact

Spring and summer come and go, and as autumn arrives, Gawain begins to think about the approach of Christmastime. He reminds King Arthur:

> Now, liege lord of my life, my leave I take;
> The terms of this task too well you know—
> To count the cost over concerns me nothing.
> But I am bound forth betimes to bear a stroke
> From the grim man in green, as God may direct.[3]

He dons his armor and with his horse, Gringolet, he sets out, traveling through northwest England. During his journey, he encounters a number of hardships. He suffers cold and hunger and must battle many beasts as he journeys into North Wales. The poem explains, "Many a cliff must he climb in country wild; / Far off from all his friends, forlorn must he ride."[4] He grows more desperate and discouraged the farther he travels.

On Christmas Day, after praying for guidance, he comes upon a splendid castle. The castle's lord, Bertilak de Hautdesert, welcomes Gawain and introduces him to his beautiful wife and an old woman. Gawain informs his hosts of his quest, saying he only has a few days before he is expected at the Green Chapel. Bertilak tells him he is within a couple miles of it, and he invites Gawain to stay and rest until then. Gawain is thankful and agrees.

Another Game

The following morning, Bertilak proposes a deal with Gawain. He offers, "A-hunting I will go / While you lie late and rest" and says he will give Gawain whatever he catches during the hunt, as long as Gawain shares with him whatever he might gain while remaining at the castle.[5] Gawain agrees and goes to bed to rest.

While Bertilak is off hunting, his wife sneaks into Gawain's bedchamber and tries to seduce him. Gawain is honorable and does not succumb to her advances. She manages to steal a kiss from Gawain. That evening, when Bertilak returns from the hunt, he presents Gawain with the deer he captured. Because Gawain got a kiss that day, he gives his host a kiss. But he does not say how he received it or who gave it to him.

The next day, while Bertilak is hunting, Lady Bertilak again enters Gawain's room. He turns down her advances, and she departs after kissing him twice. Bertilak and his men return with a boar. After dressing their game, Bertilak presents Gawain with the boar's head:

> "Now, Gawain," said the good man, "this game becomes yours
> By those fair terms we fixed, as you know full well."
> "That is true," returned the knight, "and trust me, fair friend,
> All my gains, as agreed, I shall give you forthwith."
> He clasps him and kisses him in courteous style,
> Then serves him with the same fare a second time.[6]

Gawain receives kisses from the lady of the castle.

Again, Gawain does not divulge the source of the kisses, and Bertilak is rather impressed with the young knight's profits for the day.

The third morning brings more of the same. The lady comes to Gawain and asks for a love token. Gawain refuses and turns down her offer of a gold ring. She then pleads with him to take her girdle of green silk that she wears like a belt around her waist. She claims it is charmed and has the power to protect the wearer from harm. Knowing that he must face the giant Green Knight the following day, Gawain accepts it. The lady also bestows upon him three kisses. When Bertilak returns from the hunt with a fox, Gawain kisses him three times but says nothing about the girdle he acquired from Lady Bertilak.

To the Green Chapel

The next morning, on New Year's Day, Gawain arises and dresses in all of his armor. He also puts on the girdle. He and Gringolet set off in search of the Green Chapel. A guide from Bertilak's castle leads him to the border of the forest. The guide says he will not say anything if Gawain chooses to give up his quest. But Gawain, a noble and chivalrous knight, is determined to keep his word and puts his fate in God's hands:

> *"By God," said Gawain then,*
> *"I shall not give way to weeping;*
> *God's will be done, amen!*
> *I commend me to his keeping."[7]*

He forges ahead and finds a rock crevice. Inside, he can hear a grindstone. Deciding the cavern must be the Green Chapel, he calls inside. The Green Knight comes to meet him with a freshly sharpened ax. Gawain bends and bares his neck, accepting his fate and prepared to receive his blow. The Green Knight swings once, but Gawain flinches. The Green Knight tries again, but purposely does not strike Gawain. Gawain is angered

At the end of the quest, Gawain learns more magic was at work when the Green Knight reveals himself.

with these false attempts and tells him to stop making a scene and deliver the blow. The knight swings a third time and merely scratches Gawain's neck, barely drawing blood. Gawain angrily shouts that the contract has been fulfilled and that if the Green Knight tries another blow, there will be a battle.

But the Green Knight laughs and reveals himself to be Bertilak. He had been transformed by magic, and he explains the reason he drew blood on the third blow was because Gawain deceived him on the third night and did not tell him about the green girdle he received from Lady Bertilak. Although he admonishes Gawain, stating, "True men pay what they owe," Bertilak nonetheless views Gawain as a worthy knight.[8]

Another Ruse

Bertilak further explains that the entire game was set into motion by Morgan le Faye, King Arthur's half sister and Gawain's aunt, who had posed as the old woman at the castle. Morgan, a sorceress, used her magic to transform Bertilak's appearance and sent him to test her brother's knights. Morgan has a history of causing trouble for Arthur.

Gawain feels very guilty and ashamed for having deceived Bertilak. He and the Green Knight depart on cordial terms, and Gawain returns to Camelot. There, he wears the green girdle on his arm so he won't forget that he failed to keep his oath:

> "This is the badge of false faith that I was found in there, And I must bear it on my body till I breathe my last."[9]

His fellow Knights of the Round Table welcome him home, and, to show their support, they all wear green girdles on their arms.

Failing
His Quest

*S*ir Gawain was completed within a hundred years after the failure of the last Crusade. The Crusades endeavored to reclaim the Holy Land for European Christians. Most of these holy wars were fought in Syria, Palestine, and Egypt, but particularly in Jerusalem. These wars were the ultimate real-life quest for medieval knights. The Catholic church viewed the Crusades as holy actions carried out in the name of God. The Crusades failed in 1291 with the fall of the last Christian stronghold in the Holy Land.

During the time of the Crusades, chivalry became an important ideal for knights. Knights lived by chivalry's code of brave and courteous conduct. A knight vowed to remain faithful to God, loyal to his king, and true

Europe's bloody losses during the Crusades brought aspects of chivalry into question.

to his lady. He promised to use his sword to defend the weak. He courageously faced his adversaries and was prepared to die for king and country. The chivalric code held that right would prevail over wrong, which further emboldened knights to go into battle.

The backdrop of chivalry and the Crusades is key to understanding *Sir Gawain and the Green Knight*. The poem examines the noble and brave intentions of the story's protagonist, but it ultimately illustrates the knight's failure to live by the chivalric code. The traditional quest depends on an honorable hero, but Sir Gawain proves himself lacking in chivalric morals by the end of the tale, challenging the chivalric belief that there is a clear right and wrong.

Sir Gawain's quest is driven by his sense of chivalry, which is praised throughout the poem. When

Thesis Statement

The author states the thesis. The following arguments will provide evidence to support it: "The traditional quest depends on an honorable hero, but Sir Gawain proves himself lacking in chivalric morals by the end of the tale, challenging the chivalric belief that there is a clear right and wrong."

Argument One

The author begins to argue the thesis by noting Gawain's chivalry: "Sir Gawain's quest is driven by his sense of chivalry, which is praised throughout the poem."

the Green Knight enters the hall, he challenges King Arthur or any other man who would stand in for him. When Arthur begins to approach the man to address him, Gawain nobly steps forward to take the place of his king. Knights were expected to protect their lord, and Gawain does not shy away from this duty, even though the Green Knight is mammoth in size, and Gawain knows that even if he's successful in delivering a blow to the Green Knight, he will have to receive one in return. This doesn't distract him, however, as he assures Arthur, "My body, but for your blood, is barren of worth; / And for that this folly befits not a king."[1]

Gawain's success at living out the moral code of chivalry forces him to accept the challenge that would surely be his demise. Gawain keeps his word, a defining characteristic of the chivalric code, and journeys to the Green Chapel one year later. He embarks on his quest knowing he will probably die. He bravely endures the trials and tribulations he encounters along the way, however, because he is a man of his word. According to the court's standards, a knight who possessed these qualities of honor and bravery was a true and noble knight, worthy of a heroic quest.

At the start, it seems Gawain is embarking on a standard hero's quest. Later events will complicate the story's moral.

Argument Two

Here the author points out how Gawain's morals fail him: "Sir Gawain holds to most of the rules of chivalry but ultimately fails his quest when he does not behave with honor."

Sir Gawain holds to most of the rules of chivalry but ultimately fails his quest when he does not behave with honor. Although presented with the opportunity to behave inappropriately with Lady Bertilak, he refuses to do so out of respect for his host, for the sake of the honor of the lady, and because his own morals will not allow him to do so. The lady approaches him three times in his bedchamber, and each time he stands his ground and refuses to give in to her flirtations. He is honest and honorable when he tells

Bertilak about the kisses his wife gave him. However, he lies to the Green Knight about the girdle he accepts as a gift to preserve his life. He cheated and broke his word, thereby breaking the moral code. Despite his resolute nature when turning down the advances of Lady Bertilak, he ultimately fails the test of his chivalry. Gawain has not acted nobly, cheating in order to stay alive. He allowed his fear of death to cloud his judgment and get in the way of the moral code he and his fellow knights follow.

Gawain's poor behavior before his final meeting with the Green Knight complicates the relationship between right and wrong and Gawain's heroic status in the poem. The Green Knight—the enemy—acts with mercy, a chivalric trait, while Gawain cheats and breaks the moral code. An important tenet of the code of chivalry is the belief that right will overpower wrong in the end. Throughout the course of the Crusades in the Holy Land, the Catholic Church considered the wars

Argument Three

The final argument discusses how the Green Knight's reaction muddles the poem's moral standards: "Gawain's poor behavior before his final meeting with the Green Knight complicates the relationship between right and wrong and Gawain's heroic status in the poem."

to be noble and just. Gawain believed in a chivalric code that assured him evil would not prevail. But, however justified by chivalry Gawain and the Crusades were considered to be, both failed in their endeavors.

Conclusion

In the final paragraph, the author connects the poem's morals with the Crusades and makes a final point about good and evil.

The poem's final message suggests that Gawain has learned a valuable lesson about the moral code for which he's prepared to die. Is the chivalric code always correct? Will right always prevail? What is "right," and who decides? When a knight behaves badly but the enemy acts with honor, perhaps right and wrong are no longer so clearly defined. Through *Sir Gawain*, the reader realizes, as does the protagonist, that perhaps chivalry cannot draw the line between total goodness from total evil and that there is a degree of both in everyone. Gawain becomes a more morally complicated figure than the simple hero of a quest.

Thinking Critically

Now it's your turn to assess the essay. Consider these questions:

1. Do you agree with the thesis? Why or why not?

2. How could one make the argument that *Sir Gawain* is a typical hero on a quest?

3. A conclusion should restate the thesis and main arguments. Are there any sentences in the conclusion that could be removed or simplified? Remove or modify one sentence and explain your reasoning.

Other Approaches

You have just read one possible way to consider Gawain's quest in *Sir Gawain and the Green Knight*. However, it is possible to approach the poem in different ways. One way looks at Gawain's quest as his inner quest for self-improvement. Another looks at Gawain's quest as a Christian allegory.

Seeking Self-Improvement

Sir Gawain and the Green Knight is about Gawain's physical journey and tests. But at a deeper level, it is the story of his inner quest for self-improvement. As his journey progresses, he is tested in the virtues of chivalry, including bravery, honesty, and loyalty. A thesis exploring this idea could be: Unlike many quest tales, Gawain's quest is never complete as he continues to seek self-improvement by refusing easy forgiveness and wearing the green girdle to remember his wrongdoing.

Christian Forgiveness

Seen as a Christian allegory, Gawain becomes every Christian who tries to live a moral life but sins. The Green Knight becomes a Jesus Christ figure who gives forgiveness, even as Gawain continues seeking atonement. A thesis considering the tale's religious themes could be: Gawain's quest is the quest of every Christian to lead a moral life and in the end be forgiven for his or her sins.

Analyze It!

Now that you have examined the theme of the quest, are you ready to perform your own analysis? You have read that this type of evaluation can help you look at literature in a new way and make you pay attention to certain issues you may not have otherwise recognized. So, why not look for a quest theme in one or more of your favorite books?

First, choose the work you want to analyze. What is the main quest? Are there secondary quests? Do characters grow or change through inner or moral quests? If you choose to compare the theme in more than one work, what do they have in common? How do they differ? Next, write a specific question about the theme that interests you. Then you can form your thesis, which should provide the answer to that question. Your thesis is the most important part of your analysis and offers an argument about the work, considering the theme, its effect on the characters, or what it says about society or the world. Recall that the thesis statement typically appears at the very end of the introductory paragraph of your essay. It is usually only one sentence long.

After you have written your thesis, find evidence to back it up. Good places to start are in the work itself or in journals or articles that discuss what other people have said about it. You may also want to read about the author or creator's life so you can get a sense of what factors may have affected the creative process. This can be especially useful if you are considering how the theme connects to history or the author's intent.

You should also explore parts of the book that seem to disprove your thesis and create an argument against them. As you do this, you might want to address what others have written about the book. Their quotes may help support your claim.

Before you start analyzing a work, think about the different arguments made in this book. Reflect on how evidence supporting the thesis was presented. Did you find that some of the techniques used to back up the arguments were more convincing than others? Try these methods as you prove your thesis in your own critique.

When you are finished writing your critique, read it over carefully. Is your thesis statement understandable? Do the supporting arguments flow logically, with the topic of each paragraph clearly stated? Can you add any information that would present your readers with a stronger argument in favor of your thesis? Were you able to use quotes from the book, as well as from other critics, to enhance your ideas? Did you see the work in a new light?

Glossary

absolve
To forgive or make free from guilt.

atonement
A theological concept that describes how humans are reconciled with God.

chivalry
A system of loyalty and honor followed by knights in the Middle Ages.

cornucopia
A cone-shaped container symbolizing the harvest that is filled with food and sometimes flowers.

crucifixion
A method of putting a person to death by tying or nailing him or her to a cross.

disciple
A follower of a religious figure who helps spread the doctrine to others.

dystopia
A place where everything is bad and people have terrible lives.

fascist
A type of government that is ruled by a dictator or military leader where people are not allowed to challenge the government.

gender
The state of being either male or female.

girdle
An article of clothing that encircles the body.

phial
A vial.

postapocalyptic
A period of time following an event that caused mass destruction and much loss of life.

protagonist
The main character in a book, movie, play, poem, or other work.

star-crossed
Ill-fated and seeming to have the world against it, often refers to lovers.

stereotype
An often unfair and untrue belief that many people have about all people or things with a particular characteristic—for example, gender or race.

tenet
A belief or doctrine generally accepted as truth.

Characteristics
AND CLASSICS

The quest is a common theme in literature. It is a journey—physical or mental—with a beginning, a middle, and an end. The hero is the main character of the quest story.

This theme often includes:

- A hero or heroine
- A call to action prompting the hero to leave home
- A treasure or goal at the end of the quest
- A journey through an unfamiliar place
- Challenges or obstacles the hero must overcome
- Companions or guides who assist the hero

Some famous works with a quest theme are:

- Homer's *The Odyssey*
- The myth of Hercules's 12 labors
- Virgil's *Aeneid*
- In Arthurian legend, the quest for the holy grail
- The fairy tale "East of the Sun and West of the Moon"
- Herman Melville's *Moby Dick*
- Mark Twain's *The Adventures of Huckleberry Finn*
- Lloyd Alexander's Chronicles of Prydain series
- The film *Star Wars* and its sequels
- Rick Riordan's *The Lightning Thief*
- J. K. Rowling's *Harry Potter and the Deathly Hallows*

References

Abrams, M. H., General Editor. *The Norton Anthology of English Literature, Sixth Edition, Volume I.* New York: Norton, 1993. Print.

Baum, L. Frank. *The Wonderful Wizard of Oz.* New York: Sterling, 2005. Print.

The Bible. New International Version. *Bible Gateway.* Bible Gateway, n.d. Web. 16 Jan. 2015.

Braudy, Leo, and Marshall Cohen, eds. *Film Theory and Criticism: Introductory Readings.* New York: Oxford UP, 2009. Print.

Bressler, Charles E. *Literary Criticism: An Introduction to Theory and Practice.* Upper Saddle River, NJ: Prentice Hall, 1999. Print.

Campbell, Joseph. *Hero with a Thousand Faces.* Novato, CA: New World Library, 2008. Print.

Collins, Suzanne. *The Hunger Games.* New York: Scholastic, 2008. Print.

Homer. *The Odyssey.* Trans. Robert Fagles. New York: Penguin, 1997. Print.

The Lord of the Rings: The Fellowship of the Ring. Dir. Peter Jackson. New Line Productions, New Line Home Entertainment, Inc., 2002. DVD.

The Lord of the Rings: Return of the King. Dir. Peter Jackson. New Line Productions, New Line Home Entertainment, Inc., 2004. DVD.

The Lord of the Rings: The Two Towers. Dir. Peter Jackson. New Line Productions, New Line Home Entertainment, Inc., 2003. DVD.

Lynn, Steven. *Texts and Contexts.* New York: Longman, 1997. Print.

Monaco, James. *How to Read a Film: Movies, Media and Beyond: Art, Technology, Language, History, Theory.* New York: Oxford UP, 2009. Print.

Additional
RESOURCES

Further Readings

Egan, Kate. *The World of the Hunger Games*. New York: Scholastic, 2012. Print.

Hinds, Gareth. *The Odyssey*. New York: Candlewick, 2010. Print.

Mersey, Daniel. *King Arthur*. Myths and Legends. Oxford: Osprey, 2013. Print.

Sibley, Brian. *The Lord of the Rings: The Fellowship of the Ring Insider's Guide*. New York: Houghton Mifflin, 2001. Print.

Tolkien, J. R. R. *The Fellowship of the Ring*. Reissued ed. New York: Mariner, 2012. Print.

Websites

To learn more about Essential Literary Themes, visit **booklinks.abdopublishing.com**. These links are routinely monitored and updated to provide the most current information available.

Places to Visit

**The Academy of Motion Picture Arts
and Sciences Museum**
8949 Wilshire Boulevard
Beverly Hills, CA 90211
310-247-3000
http://www.oscars.org
The museum embraces the interdisciplinary approach of
filmmaking and how it combines theater, literature, photography,
painting, music, and other art forms.

The Birmingham Tolkien Trail and Sarehole Mill
Cole Bank Road, Hall Green
Birmingham B13 0BD
England
0121-348-8160
http://www.birminghammuseums.org.uk
Sarehole Mill provided inspiration for Tolkien's Shire. An annual
Tolkien Weekend event celebrates his life and works.

**The International L. Frank Baum and All Things Oz
Historical Foundation**
219 Genesee Street
Chittenango, NY 13037
315-333-2286
http://www.allthingsoz.com
The foundation promotes education on the writings of L. Frank
Baum and provides a large collection of items from the author's
life.

Source Notes

Chapter 1. Introduction to Themes in Literature

None.

Chapter 2. An Overview of *The Wonderful Wizard of Oz*

1. L. Frank Baum. *The Wonderful Wizard of Oz*. New York: Sterling, 2005. Print. 4.
2. Ibid. 64.
3. Ibid. 149.
4. Ibid. 150.
5. Ibid. 153.
6. Ibid. 153.

Chapter 3. Women on Quests

1. L. Frank Baum. *The Wonderful Wizard of Oz*. New York: Sterling, 2005. Print. 21.

Chapter 4. An Overview of *The Hunger Games*

1. Suzanne Collins. *The Hunger Games*. New York: Scholastic, 2008. Print. 19.
2. Ibid. 146.
3. Ibid. 342.

Chapter 5. The Flawed Mentor

1. Suzanne Collins. *The Hunger Games*. New York: Scholastic, 2008. Print. 46–47.
2. Ibid. 56.
3. Ibid. 57.
4. Ibid. 58.
5. Ibid. 117.

Chapter 6. An Overview of
the Lord of the Rings Trilogy

1. *The Lord of the Rings: The Fellowship of the Ring.* Dir. Peter Jackson. New Line Productions, New Line Home Entertainment, Inc., 2002. DVD.

2. Ibid.

3. *The Lord of the Rings: The Return of the King.* Dir. Peter Jackson. New Line Productions, New Line Home Entertainment, Inc., 2004. DVD.

4. Ibid.

Chapter 7. A Religious Journey

1. *The Bible.* New International Version. *Bible Gateway.* Bible Gateway, n.d. Web. 16 Jan. 2015. Luke 22:42.

2. Ibid. Luke 4:40.

3. *The Lord of the Rings: The Fellowship of the Ring.* Dir. Peter Jackson. New Line Productions, New Line Home Entertainment, Inc., 2002. DVD.

4. Ibid.

5. Ibid.

Chapter 8. An Overview of
Sir Gawain and the Green Knight

1. M. H. Abrams, General Editor. *The Norton Anthology of English Literature, Sixth Edition, Volume I.* New York: Norton, 1993. Print. 206. Lines 209–214.

2. Ibid. 211. Line 48.

3. Ibid. 213. Lines 545–549.

4. Ibid. 217. Lines 713–714.

5. Ibid. 225. Lines 1101–1102.

6. Ibid. 236. Lines 1635–1640.

7. Ibid. 246. Lines 2156–2159.

8. Ibid. 250. Line 2354.

9. Ibid. 253. Lines 2509–2510.

Chapter 9. Failing His Quest

1. M. H. Abrams, General Editor. *The Norton Anthology of English Literature, Sixth Edition, Volume I.* New York: Norton, 1993. Print. 209. Lines 357–358.

Index

About the Author

Susan E. Hamen has written numerous children's books on various topics, including the Wright brothers, Pearl Harbor, World War II, the Industrial Revolution, and engineering. Her book *Clara Barton: Civil War Hero and American Red Cross Founder* made the American Library Association's 2011 Amelia Bloomer Project Book List. Hamen lives in Minnesota with her husband and two children. Her favorite activities include traveling with her family, reading with her kids, and spending time around the campfire on chilly autumn nights.